Inside a Dorze hut, Chencha

ETHIOPIA

inspiring journey

Sunrise on the way to the village of Sof Omar, Bale.

Welcome to ETHIOPIA.

A collection of Ethiopia's inspiring people, places, cultures, and landscapes.

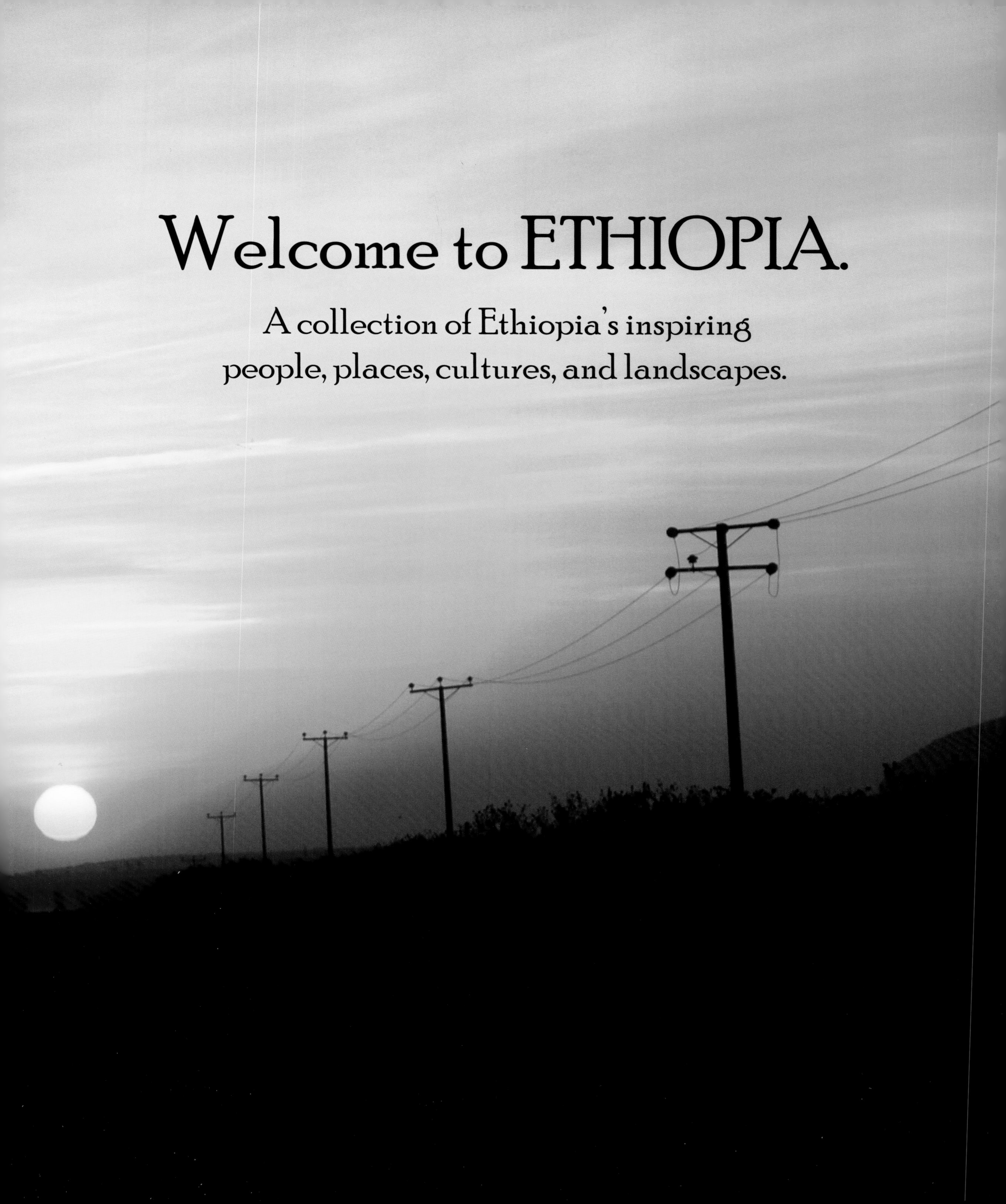

infoAddis Publishing, LLC
P.O.Box 10819
Alexandria, VA 22310
www.infoAddis.com

ISBN: 978-0-9856829-0-3

Created by infoAddis Publishing, LLC. A great deal of effort was exerted to limit errors and omissions. Nevertheless, the publisher cannot accept responsibility for errors, omissions, or the consequences of any reliance of the information provided.

3000 Years of History
85 Million Smiles

HISTORIC ROUTE

Ethiopia is the oldest independent country in Africa. The discovery of Lucy, a 3.2-million-year-old skeleton connects Ethiopia to the very beginnings of humanity. The rich history of Ethiopia makes it a unique and rewarding place to visit. Tourists who are interested in the history of the country are encouraged to take a path designed to highlight the ancient civilization of Axum, the architectural wonders of Lalibela, and the imposing castles of Gonder.

This section features: Axum, a clear indication of advanced ancient civilization – Axum Tsion Maryam: The Chapel of the Tablet, the sanctuary of the original Ark of the Covenant – The ancient ruins of Queen of Sheba's Palace – Abraha Astibaha, a 10th-century monastery – Debre Damo Monastery, a sign of magnificent devotion – The Adwa Mountains, where Ethiopia defeated the Italian army – Lalibela, a town of architectural wonders – Asheten Maryam and Ne-Akute Le-Abe , hidden jewels of Christianity – Abune Eyesus Moa Monastery in Hayk , a place to witness the lifelong dedication of monks and nuns. – Castles in Gonder – Sof Omar Caves, spectacular underground caverns – Rimbaud Centre: A museum in Harar dedicated to the life of poet Arthur Rimbaud.

The Obelisks of Axum

Axum

Axum is a city in northern Ethiopia. The significance of Axum is embedded in the daily lives of the Ethiopian Orthodox Christians. The city houses the Tabot, the original Ark of the Covenant, the Palace of the Queen of Sheba, ancient obelisks, and the tombs of Kings Kaleb and Gebre Meskel of Axum.

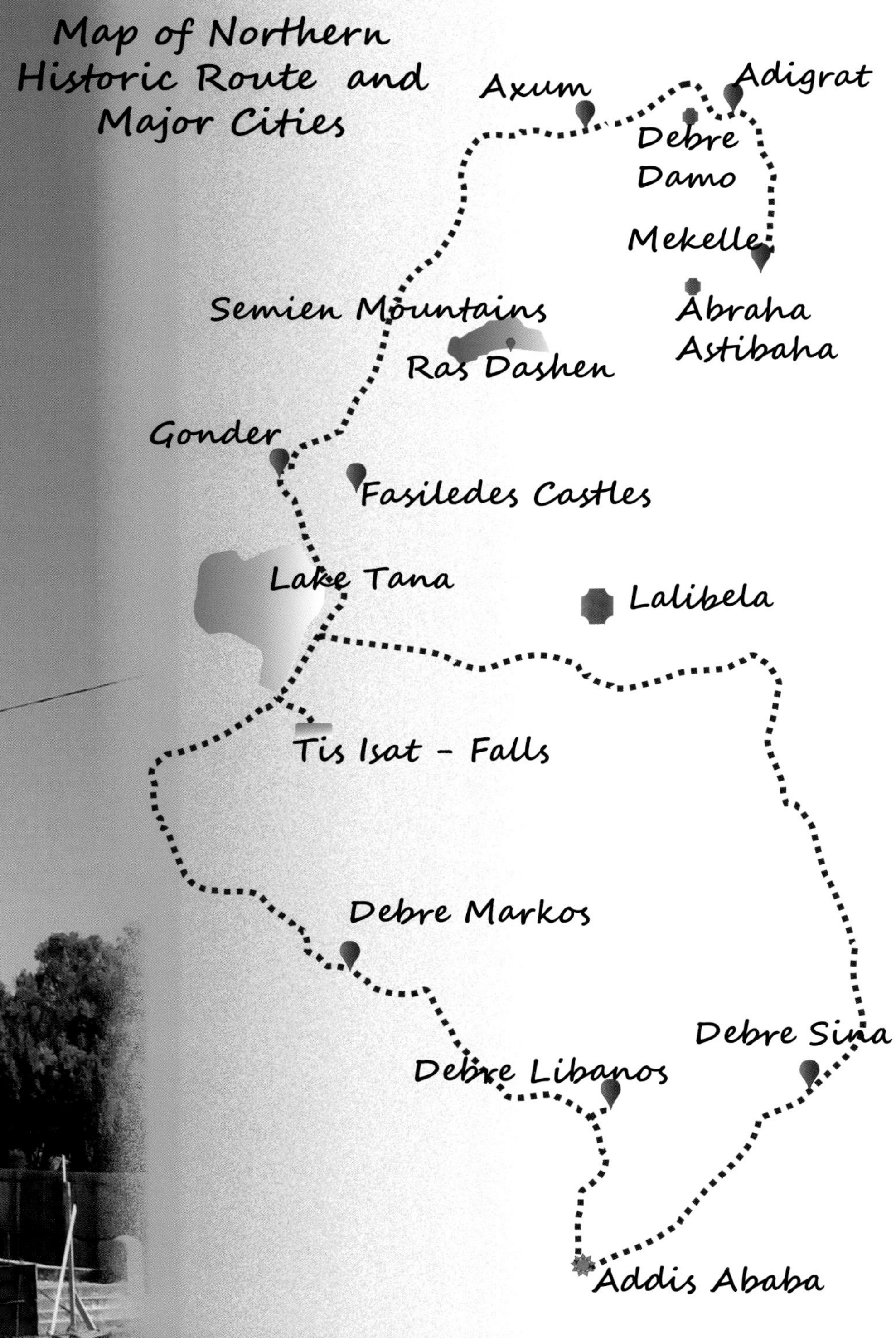

Axum Tsion Maryam

The Tsion Maryam (Church of St. Mary of Zion) is a unique and historical location with immense importance, as it is the Sanctuary for the original Ark of the Covenant. The Ark, which is said to have come to Ethiopia with Menelik I after visiting his father, King Solomon, is guarded and viewed by a single monk. The guardian monk is appointed for life by his predecessor.

Left: Mural inside Tsion Maryam – Opposite: The sanctuary to the original Ark of the Covenant – Below: Inside the Tsion Maryam compound.

The Chapel of the Tablet
Sanctuary to the original Ark of the Covenant

Ruins of Queen of Sheba's Palace

Makeda, who became the Queen of Sheba, was a strong-willed woman of bold character. She traveled to Jerusalem to meet King Solomon, and their rendezvous produced a son named Menelik (I), which started the Solomonic dynasty in Ethiopia. Panoramas of the ruins of Makeda's palace leave Axum's visitors with a slice of history.

Abraha Astibaha

Right and below

Abraha Astibaha is a semi-monolithic, rock-hewn, 10th-century monastery located in Tigray. The inside of the church is simple and richly decorated with 17th- and 18th-century murals.

Debre Damo Monastery

Debre Damo is a monastery located on a plateau about 90 kilometers northeast of Axum. The founder of Debre Damo, Abune Aregawi, was said to have been provided with a large serpent to help him make the 15-meter climb up a sheer cliff required to reach the summit. To this day visitors are challenged to mimic his climb with the aid of a rope.

The location of Debre Damo Monastery relative to major northern cities

Debre Damo Monastery from a distance.

Entrance to the Debre Damo Monastery

Above: Off road entrance sign to the Debre Damo Monastery. Right: Wooden ceiling decorated with carved animals inside Abune Aregawi church, Debre Damo. Below: Murals depicting Abune Aregawi and the serpent.

In 1896, the Ethiopian people, led by King Menelik II, defeated the invading Italian army in the mountains of Adwa. The impressive victory secured Ethiopia's reputation as a resister of colonization.

Bete Giyorgis
Church of Saint George in Lalibela

Lalibela

Lalibela is a city filled with mysterious and beautiful churches, each hewn by hand from a single rock. Entering the churches will make you appreciate the resolve required to excavate with such precision.

A Lalibela priest reciting his daily prayers.

Lalibela priest holding distinctive styles of the Ethiopian crosses.

Praying in Lalibela

Asheten Maryam priest showing one of the church's ancient hand illustrated manuscript.

Asheten Maryam

Asheten Maryam is a 13th-century monastery located in the mountain atop the town of Lalibela. Reaching the church requires considerable stamina and determination. An early morning start is recommended to reach the summit before the conclusion of service.

Ne-Akute Le-Abe

also spelled Na'akuto La'ab

Ne-Akute Le-Abe is a church built under a natural cave. It is located a short distance from the city of Lalibela. The church's dripping holy water is collected into rock pots before being distributed to believers.

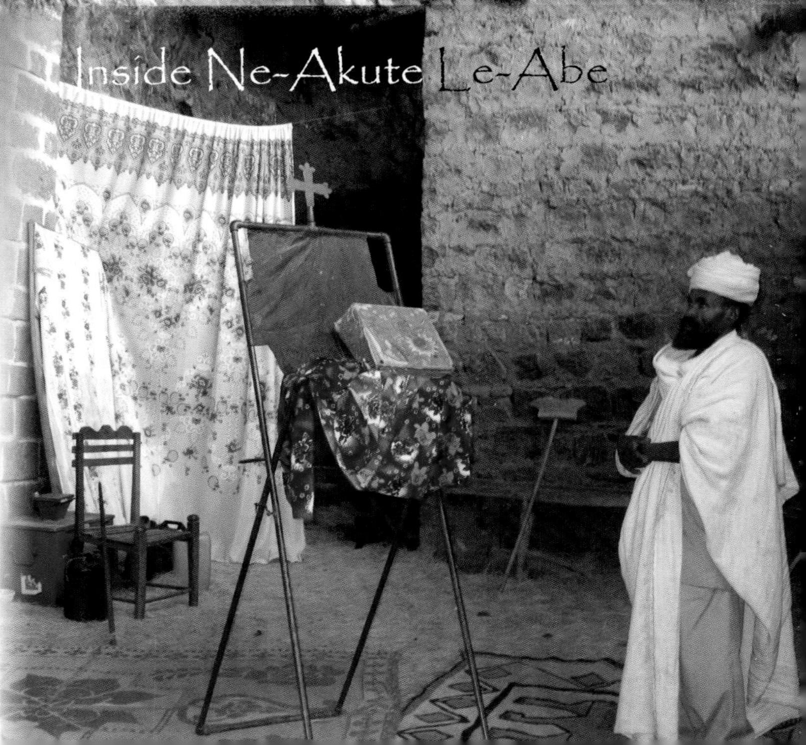

Inside Ne-Akute Le-Abe

Lalibela priest holding distinctive styles of the Ethiopian crosses.

Hayk and Abune Eyesus Monastery in Wello

Located between Dessie and Wichale, the city of Hayk is known for its monasteries and beautiful landscapes. The self-sufficient monks and nuns strive to grow plants and make materials they require for their daily needs. A stop at the Abune Eyesus Monastery and Kidane Mehret Nunnery's gift shop can be a rewarding experience

Opposite: Monks inside Abune Eyesus Moa Monastery performing their daily activities. Below: Hayk Lake seen from inside the Abune Eyesus Moa Monastery.

Gonder

Situated in the foothills of the Semien Mountains, Gonder has earned the epithet "Camelot of Africa." The city was King Fasiledes' chosen capital from 1635 to 1667. The Royal Enclosure located near the center of the city houses the impressive castles. A trip to Gonder is a must if you wish to witness a prime example of power, authority, and majesty. Visitors will also appreciate the 17th-century murals decorating Debre Berhan Selassie Church.

King Fasiledes' Palace

Emperor Iyasu's Palace in Fasiledes' Royal Enclosure, Gonder

Empress Mentwabe's (front) and Emperor Yohannes' (back) Palaces in Fasiledes' Royal Enclosure, Gonder

Sof Omar Caves

The spectacular underground caverns are found near the small village of Sof Omar about 120 kilometers from the town of Goba, Bale. The caverns are an important Islamic shrine.

Sof Omar Caves

Homes near the entrance of
The Sof Omar Caves

Arthur Rimbaud Center in Harar

The poet Arthur Rimbaud's home, located inside the walled city of Harar, is used as a museum dedicated to his life. The dated pictures hanging on the first-floor walls give visitors a window into the old city of Harar. The colorfully stained glass windows throughout the house bring contrast to the art and photos inside.

Arthur Rimbaud Center in Harar

NATURE

Visiting Ethiopia's vast natural beauty is like immersing yourself in imagination. The remarkable lakes, falls, mountains, and valleys are beyond what a wide-angle lens can capture. Ethiopia is undoubtedly one of Mother Nature's high-quality stores. From the beautiful year-round weather to the lush and picturesque landscapes, it is showered with breathtaking compositions. The native animals further enrich visits to places like the Bale Mountains National Park.

This section features: A bird of prey, Sanetti Plateau – A marabou from Amora Gedel, Awassa – Various animals from the Nech Sar National Park – Ethiopian Wolf and Nyala from the Bale Mountains – A local medicinal tree – Protective Warthog – Flamingos on lake Abijatta – Ostrich Farm – Lions in Addis Ababa Zoo – Portraits of Vervet and Colobus monkeys – Pelicans and marabous.

Bird of prey taking off from Sanetti Plateau, Bale

Amora Gedel, Awassa.

A marabou showing off for spectators by spreading its wings to their fullest.

Nech Sar National Park

Nech Sar National Park is home to picturesque lakes and a variety of animals. Lake Chamo, one of the two lakes in the park, is where you will find the famous crocodile gathering place known as Azo Gebeya.

Nech Sar National Park
and Surroundings
Lake Abaya
Chencha
Arba Minch
Nech Sar
National Park
Lake Chamo

Ethiopian Wolf (Key Kebero), Bale Mountains

Mountain Nyala

Bale National Park

Above: The graceful Mountain Nyala, unique to Ethiopia, poses for a perfect portrait.

Right: Female Nyala reacting to a sense of danger.

A Hagenia Abyssinica (kosso) tree is abundant in the highlands of the Ba
Mountains. The tree is known for its medicinal use to combat human tapewor

Bale Mountain warthog, intuitively entering into a protective mode

Flamingos on Lake Abijatta

Ostrich Farm

Langano Ostrich Farm is located in a fenced-in portion of the Abijatta-Shalla Lakes National Park near Langano.

Above: Lions in Addis Ababa Zoo. Opposite: Vervet monkey modeling for visitors while Colobus monkey showing off equal talent with side profile poses.

Amora Gedel - Lake Awassa

The best place for close-up look at pelicans (above) and marabous (below).

LANDSCAPES

Ethiopia offers an abundance of picturesque landscapes. The combination of frequent clear weather, natural architecture, and abundant observation points can easily help you lose yourself in nature.

This section features: Konso Living – Sebsebe Washa – Abay Bridge – Swimming in Konso – Lake Awassa – Near Sebsebe Washa – Sunset and granite plug in Gonder – Villages around Lake Abijatta-Shalla – Bizet, Tigray – Around Dorze village – Tis Isat Falls – Jacaranda trees – Termite towers near Yabelo – Traditional wooden beehives – Birds in Arba Minch – Lake Abaya , Chamo and Nech Sar Park – Homes near Lake Abijatta – Lake Koka – Crossing the Omo River – The town of Omorate – "New York" in Konso – Sanetti Plateau – Serenity in Awash – Salt mining in Chew Bahir – Looking over escarpment near Debre Sina

Konso Living

Sebsebe Washa

A limestone outcrop near Dinsho, Bale Mountains.

Abay Bridge

Across the Blue Nile River in Gojam.

Natural swimming pool near Konso

Lake Awassa

Near Sebsebe Washa, Bale at 2900m elevation.

Sunset at the outskirts of Gonder

Granite plug near Gonder

Opposite: Various landscape pictures of northern Ethiopia
Below: Families near Abijatta-Shalla Lakes National Park, fetching wood used to build fire for cooking.

Bizet, Tigray

Above and Opposite: Various landscape pictures of Dorze villages.

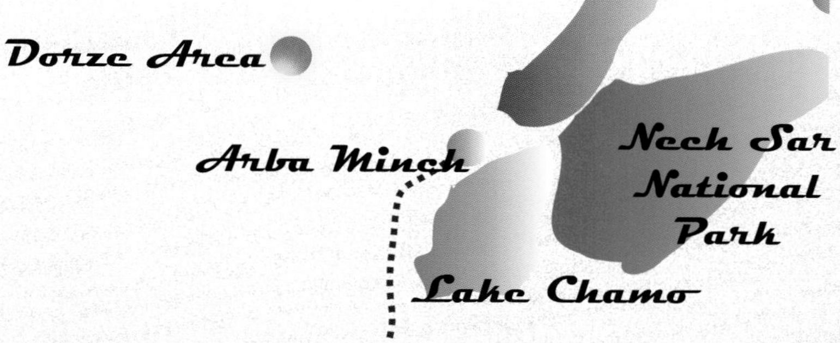

The Tis Isat Falls is a waterfall on the Blue Nile River near the city of Bahir Dar. Although the photo was taken during the fall's low volume, the absolute power illustrated by the overall scene is fascinating. A close-up look at the falls is needed to properly absorb the majestic power and beauty.

Purple Jacaranda trees in Bahir Dar.

Termite towers (Kuyisa) near Yabelo

Traditional wooden beehives hanging from an acacia tree are a common sight in the Dorze village.

Birds taking advantage of the early morning sunshine in Arba Minch

Lake Abaya and Nech Sar National Park.

Homes near Lake Abijatta.

Free-range livestock near Koka Reservoir and Dam.

Crossing the Omo River

The town of Omorate is located in southern Ethiopia near the Kenyan border. Access to the town requires crossing the Omo River via a dugout canoe. The short canoe journey to the town is as interesting as the people you'll encounter when you arrive.

The town of Omorate

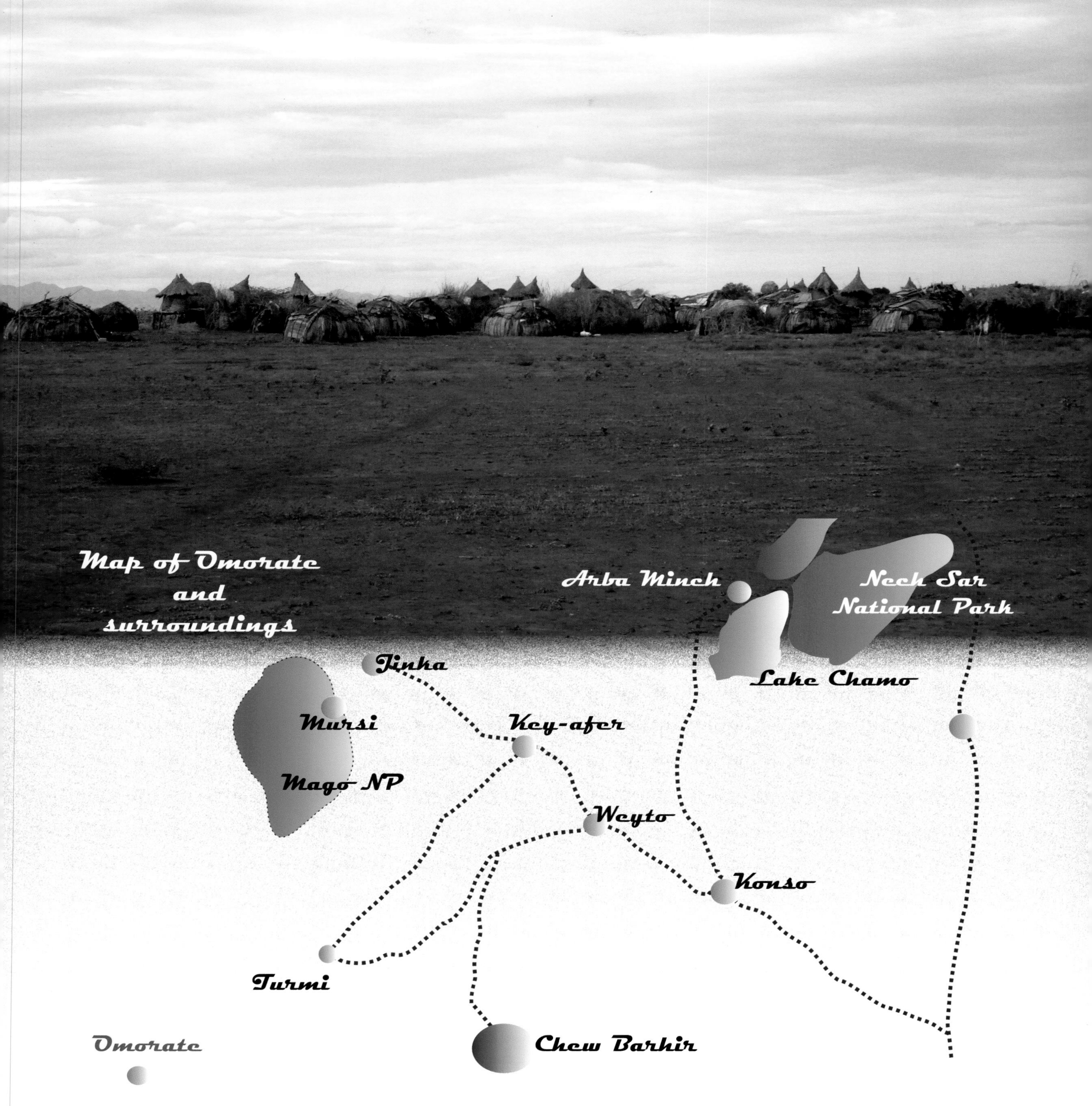

Konso: The natural mud towers sculpted by the occasional water flow resemble a city filled with skyscrapers. Reflecting this phenomenon, the area is nicknamed "New York."

Everlasting flowers and ice found on the Sanetti Plateau of the Bale Mountains.

Awash

When traveling from Addis Ababa, Awash is an ideal place to enjoy a breather before heading to Harar and Dire Dawa. The tranquility of the river will captivate your eyes, sending you on an unsuccessful search for the point of origin.

A whirlwind forming near Awash

Chew Bahir

Chew Bahir and
surrounding towns

Opposite: Chew Bahir

Chew Bahir is a salty crater located in southern Ethiopia. With the assistance of a pole, working men use their feet to gather the salt to a central location. The salt is then retrieved manually from the bottom of the crater. Endurance is a must if you wish to complete the two-hour round-trip hike for a closer look.

RELIGIONS

Ethiopians practice a variety of religions, but most are Orthodox Christians or Muslims. The influence of Christianity in Ethiopia is expansive and is reflected in daily social and cultural behaviors.

This section features: Murals from Churches in Lake Tana – Carved stone in Bete Gologotha, Lalibela – Epiphany (Timket) celebration in Addis Ababa – Shek Sof Omar Shrine – Mosques in Kombolcha, Dodola and Debre Zeyit – Holy Trinity Cathedral in Addis Ababa – 17th century murals in Debre Berhan Selassie Church, Gonder – Exterior of the Debre Berhan Selassie Church – A cross from Lake Tana's ancient churches and monasteries – Exterior view of the new Church of Tsion Maryam in Axum – Crowns of former Ethiopian Emperors – Ancient hand illustrated manuscript – Ethiopian Orthodox prayer sticks – Bole Medhanialem, Ethiopian Orthodox Church in Addis Ababa.

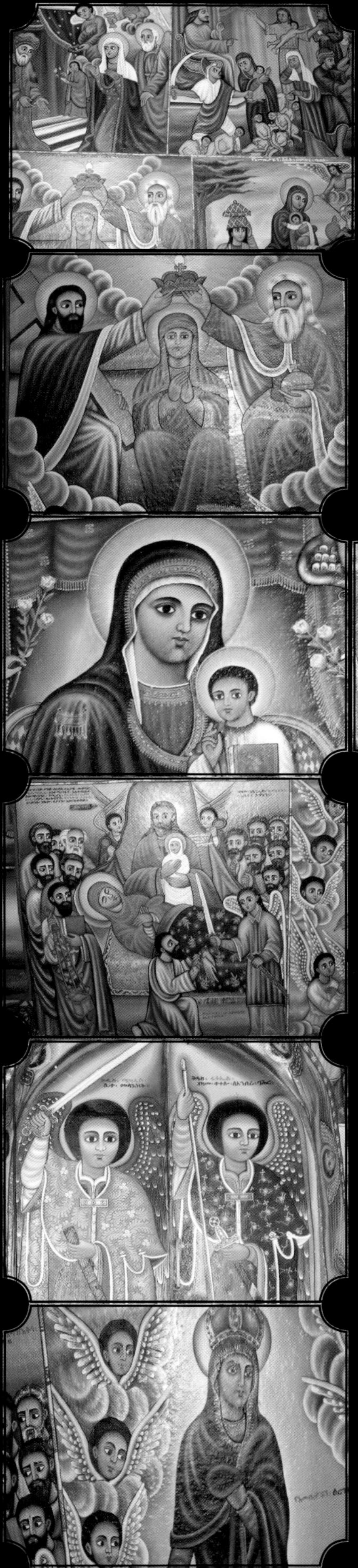

Murals from Churches i
Lake Tana

Carved stone in Bete Gologotha, Lalibela

Epiphany (Timket) celebration in Addis Ababa

Looking out from Shek Sof Omar Shrine cave

Modern mosque in Kombolcha, Wello

Mosque in Addis Ababa

Left: Mosque near Debre Zeyit.

Below: Mosque near Dodola, Bale.

Opposite: 17th century murals in Debre Berhan Selassie Church, Gonder.
Inset: exterior.

Below: Holy Trinity Cathedral in Addis Ababa.

Above: Exterior view of the Church of Tsion Maryam in Axum.
Opposite: A cross from Lake Tana's ancient churches and monasteries.
Below: Crowns of former Ethiopian Emperors located in Tsion Maryam.

Opposite: Hand illustrated manuscript inside Ne-Akute Le-Abe church in Lalibela.

Below: Ethiopian Orthodox prayer sticks serve a dual purpose: used to lean on during services and as a liturgical instrument in sacred hymn and dance.

Bole Medhanialem,
Ethiopian Orthodox Church in Addis Ababa

CULTURES

This section includes pictures of cultural events and ordinary practices around the country. The assembly of an early morning market in Chencha and the cultural dance and bull-jumping ceremony of the Hamer people are examples of some of the unscripted and magnificent events included below.

This section features: Dorze home – Making Kocho bread – Dorze weavers – Early morning market in Chencha – The Hamar – Bull jumping – Evangadi – Dancing for the Ukuli – Town elder – Leg of a cow – The Mursi People – Cultural shows – Inside Adare home in Harar.

Opposite page: Dorze homes are tall, unique structures, built with vertical hardwood poles and woven bamboos. The houses are intentionally built high, up to 12 meters, to compensate for the inevitable termite damage to the lower sections. After careful examinations, locals remove the spoiled lower sections and reuse the rest of the house. Therefore, the older the house, the shorter it is.

A Dorze woman making Kocho (bread) from the roots of a false banana tree. Part of the plant is isolated, pulverized, and fermented before being used to make the Kocho bread.

DORZE VILLAGE

Above: Aided by balmy weather and natural backdrop, Dorze weavers concentrate on the product of the day.

Chencha

Tuesday morning open market assembling in Chencha,
Guge Mountain.

The Hamer

One of the groups in the lower Omo valley, the Hamer people are known for their elaborate attire, cultural ceremonies, and unpretentious pride.

Bull Jumping

A successful bull-jumping is a sign of a Hamer boy's coming of age. A number of bulls are lined up and restrained from the slightest of movements to allow the *ukuli* (man-to-be) to make the jump. If successful, he becomes a *maz.*

. Preparing the bulls

2. Maz leading the way

. Marching to the jump location

4. Arriving at the jump location

He is now a **maz**, part of the Hamer adult society ready to accept such responsibilities as marriage.

After a successful social leap from youth to adulthood, a celebration is in order. The next evening, the feast and dance commence. The event is known as *evangadi*.

A dancing ceremony in honor of the Ukuli

A Hamer lady transporting leg of a cow protected by fresh eucalyptus leaves

Opposite: A Hamer town elder returning from witnessing The Bull Jumping Ceremony carrying his headrest and rifle.

The Mursi people are located in the Mago National Park in southern Ethiopia.

A map of Mursi and the surrounding towns

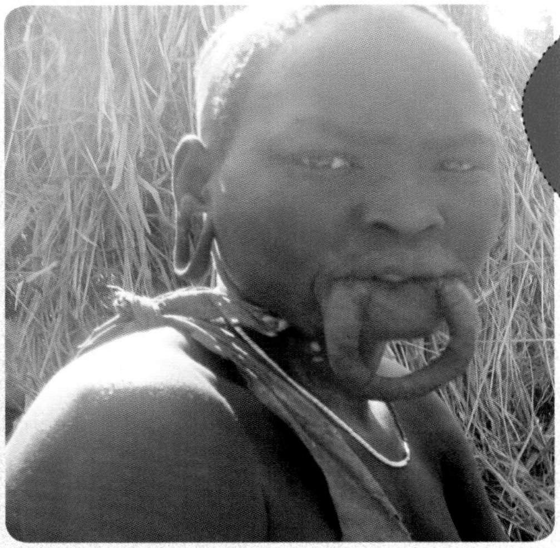

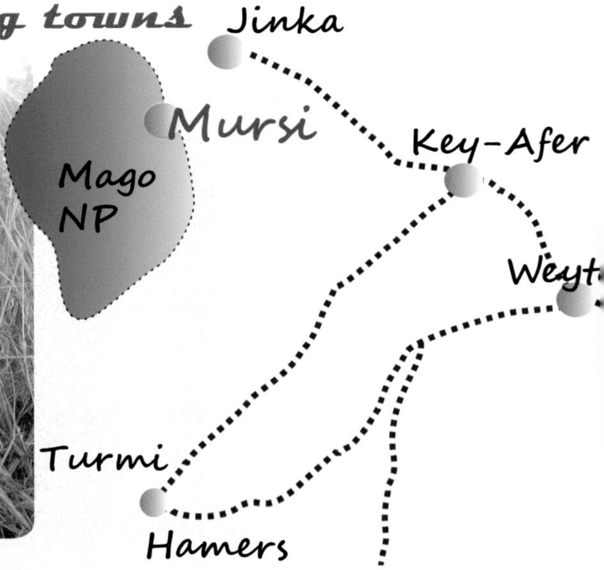

The Mursi women are known for their practice of wearing a lip plate. As girls in the tribe, they begin by inserting billets of wood to their lower lip; the lip gradually stretches to accommodate such clay plates shown in the pictures.

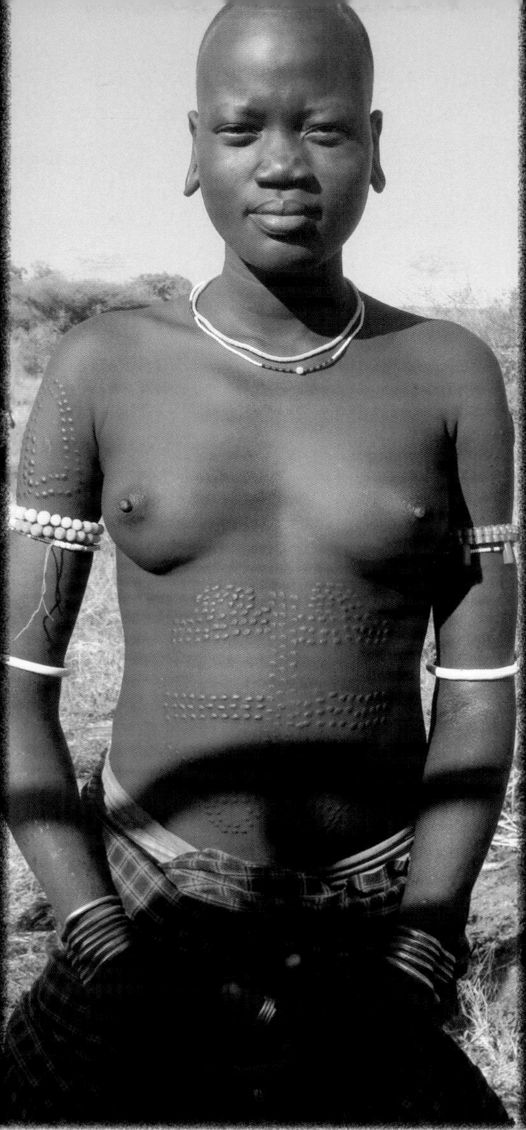

There are more than 70 ethnic groups in Ethiopia. Each group has its own distinctive rhythm and styles of dancing. Professional performers frequently display these styles in selected Addis Ababa restaurants, where diners enjoy authentic traditional food in cultural settings.

Cultural show in Crown Hotel, Addis Ababa.

Inside a model of a traditional Adare home.
The National Cultural Centre, Harar.

PEOPLE

One advantage of Ethiopia's diverse cultures is its people's equally distinct ways of life. This section of the book highlights the various people encountered throughout the country.

A lady from Omorate
outfitted with
homemade jewelry

Ethiopia is the birthplace of coffee. For many, drinking coffee is an entrenched routine in their daily lives. Ethiopians' love affair for coffee is illustrated by the unique and welcoming ceremony. The ceremony starts by roasting the green coffee beans over open-air brazier before grinding them with a wooden mortar and pestle. Jebena, a traditional Ethiopian coffee pot, is then used to brew the coffee to perfection. The brewing process starts by warming up cold water in the coffee pot. Just the right amount of coffee is then added and the mixture is allowed to boil slowly. The experienced brewer times the procedure and uses a skillful touch to make sure the grounds are settled before the precious brew is served in demitasse cups.

Helping mom fetch wood used to build fire
for cooking , Goba

Above: friendships in Omorate

Below: friendships in Abijatta

Young ladies of Borena.

Above: A clear sign of hospitality from the Hamer land.

Opposite: The Hamer ladies rub a mixture of red ochre, water, and animal fat in their hair before braiding it . The result is a colorful hair style that compliments their homemade

A priest from Axum, heading to Tsion Maryam Church.

Ethiopian Orthodox priests and deacons during Epiphany (Timket) celebration in Addis Ababa

Locals heading to Tuesday market in Weldiya, Wello

The art of weaving is a widely practiced tradition throughout Ethiopia. The Dorzes are especially known for their proficiency in the art and the superior quality of their finished products. The process starts with the refining of cotton and ends with clothing for local consumption.

Ring-necked doves on Sanetti Plateau, Bale

Locals use horses to get around the rugged terrain of the Bale Mountains.

Lifelong friendships in Konso

Street view near Menelik II Secondary School, Addis Ababa.

Far Left: Goba woman heading home after a long day at the market.

Middle: Goba man checking on the health of his transportation.

Right: Goba market in action.

Below: Horse parking near Goba market in Bale.

A home on the highlands of Bale.

MONTAGE

Most towns and villages in Ethiopia have designated days for local markets. The dynamic nature of all markets makes them prime places to visit. Some people travel long distances to market goods, while others casually stroll to bask in the energy of the market scene.

Above: General markets in Goba and Chencha
Bellow: Sheep market in Addis Ababa.

Above: Household market in Turmi.
Below: Early morning bamboo market in Goba, Bale.

Friendships

Cultural dance performer at Crown Hotel, wearing one of the many styles of hand-woven traditional dresses. The complimentary embroidery and waist-tie enhance her appearance.

Traditional gojo houses near the town of Shashemene

HOMES

Most people in Ethiopia's remote towns and villages live in mud huts, or *gojo*. The design varies from a single room with one door to more elaborate multi-room structures with high ceilings.

Gojo near the town of Mojo

Sof Omar

Mursi

Lalibela

Ethiopian Orthodox Christianity followers believe in the healing power of the Holy Water. They often hang containers filled with it outside their rooms.

Lewi Resort.

Entrance to the Harar Cultural Center

Cities, Towns and Villages

A quick stop or overnight stay in Ethiopia's cities, towns, and villages gives travelers the opportunity to experience the country's fabled hospitality.

Yabelo

Sof Omar

Harar

Dire Dawa

Addis Ababa

Addis Ababa is the modern and vibrant capital city of Ethiopia. The city is also Africa's choice for the African Union headquarters. "New flower," as the name translates, is often referred to as the political capital of Africa.

Sheraton Addis, a luxury collection hotel in Addis Ababa

Tewodros Adebabay

A circle dedicated to Atse Tewodros, Emperor of Ethiopia from 1855 - 1868 . At the center of the circle is a replica of the cannon the emperor used to strengthen his military might.

Dila

Konso

Asebe Tefere

Hageremariam

Shashemene

Wokro

Kombolcha

Dessie

Weldia

Lalibela

Awassa

Goba

Asela

Bahir Dar

Yirga Chefe

Adigrat

Gotera, the recently completed underpass bridge in Addis Ababa.

Tending farms

Agriculture is the foundation of Ethiopia's economy. Over 80 percent of the population is engaged in agricultural production.

Sinana Agricultural Development in Bale

Acknowledgments

You inspire me to strive higher.

Addisalem
Abiel
Joseph

Thank you for your continued support.

Family and Friends

Your time and effort are greatly appreciated

Alehubel Teshome
Alula Kebede
Ayele Gugssa
Bekele Berhanu
Dawit Lakew
Desalenge Mekonnen
Elias Meshesha
Fisseha Damte
Fukare Yimtatu
Hanna & Manfred Salamon
Hilemariam Gizaw
Kebere Assefa
Kedeme Oda
Lulit Ayne
Myrna McCullin
Sebhat Abdela
Senedu Araya-Sellassie
Teddy Tadesse
Yared Negash
Yemeru Tessema
Zewdie Guadie

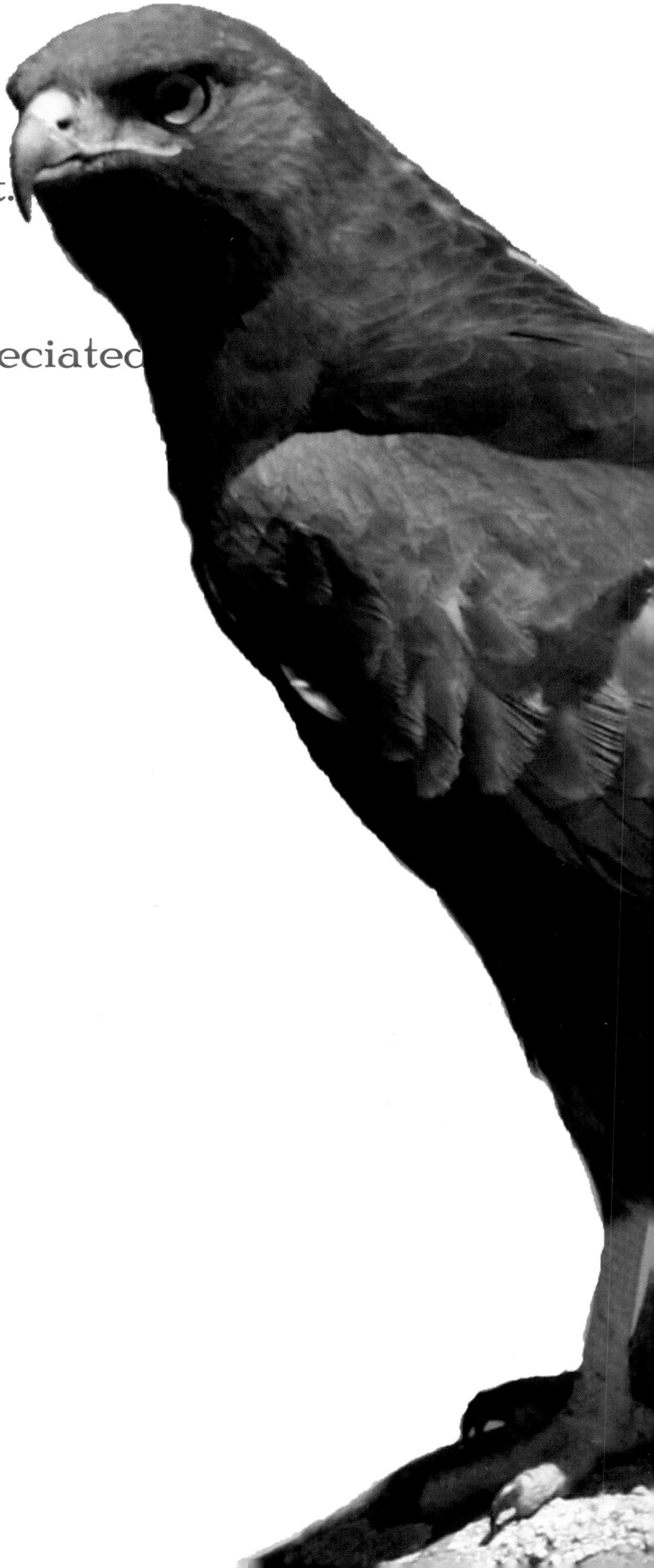

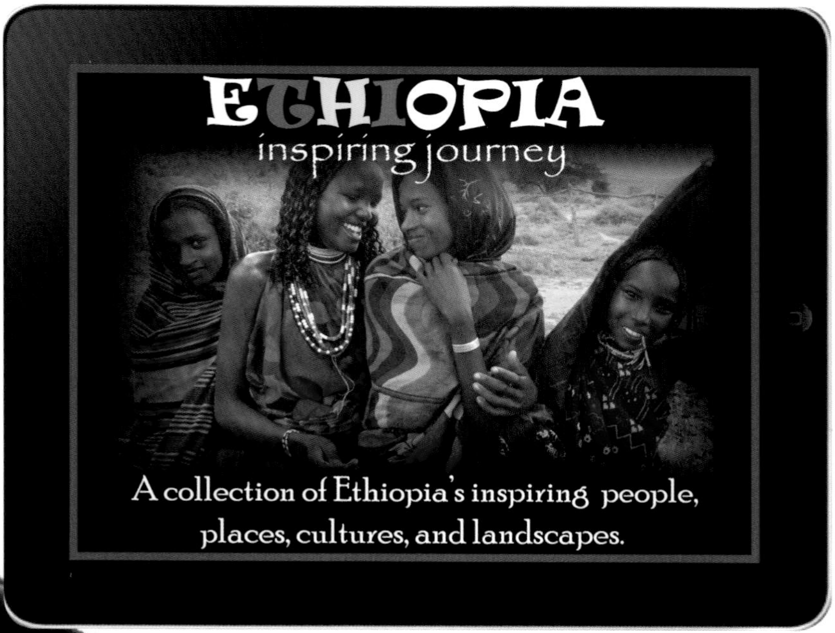

A bird of prey, Sanetti Plateau, Bale

index

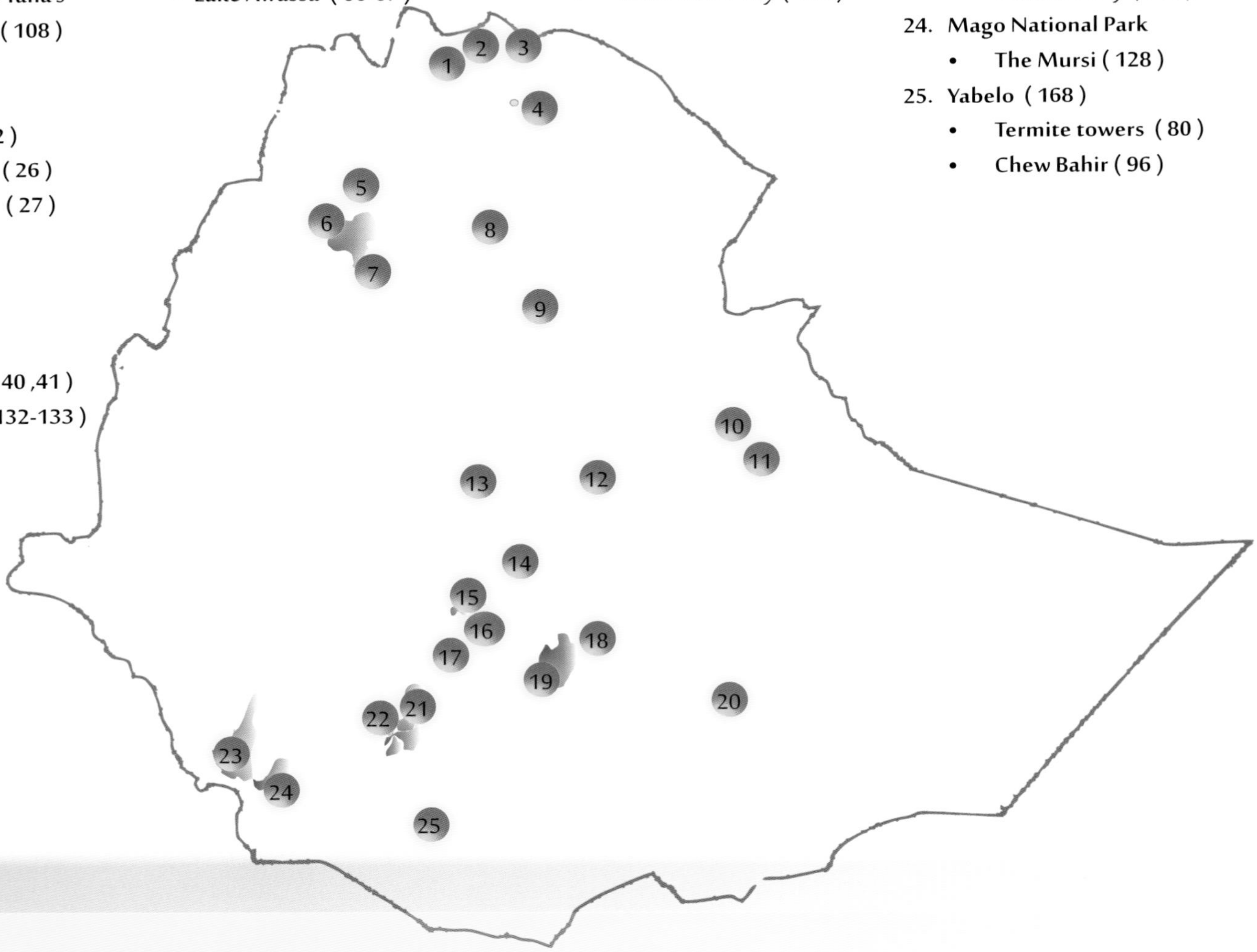

Inside a Dorze hut, Chencha